Colours

Written by Sally Morgan

CRISS X CROSS

Bodies	Fairgrounds	Light	Special Days
Boxes	Growth	Patterns	Textures
Changes	Holes	Rubbish	Weather
Colours	Journeys	Senses	Wheels

Picture acknowledgements

The publishers would like to thank the following for allowing their photographs to be reproduced in this book: Cephas 23 (Mick Rock), 24 (above/Peter O'Neill); ECOSCENE frontispiece (Lees), 5 (above/Morgan), 6 (Cooper), 7 (above/Morgan), 7 (below/Brown), 8 (above/Farmar), 8 (below), 9 (Payne), 10 (both above/Cooper), 10 (below/Whitty), 11, 12 (above/Greenwood), 12 (below/Harwood), 13 (above/Gryniewicz), 13 (below/Greenwood), 14 (Cooper), 15 (above/Adams), 15 (below/Towse), 16 (above/Morgan), 16 (below/Purslow), 17 (Cooper), 22 (above/Cooper), 22 (below/Lees), 24 (below/Winkley), 25 (above/Towse), 26 (above), 28 (Lillicrap), 29 (above/Morgan), 29 (below/Winkley); Wayland Picture Library 4, 5, 18 (both), 19 (both), 20 (below), 26 (below), 27 (both); ZEFA 20 (above), 21, 25 (below).

**Cover photography by Daniel Pangbourne, organized by Zoë Hargreaves.
With thanks to the Fox Primary School.**

First published in 1993 by
Wayland (Publishers) Ltd
61 Western Road, Hove
East Sussex BN3 1JD, England

© Copyright 1993 Wayland (Publishers) Ltd

Editor: Francesca Motisi
Designers: Jean and Robert Wheeler

Consultant: Alison Watkins is an experienced teacher with a special interest in language and reading. She has been a class teacher but at present is the special needs coordinator for a school in Hackney. Alison wrote the notes for parents and teachers and provided the topic web.

British Library Cataloguing in Publication Data
Morgan Sally.
Colours. – (Criss Cross Series)
I. Title II. Series
535.6

ISBN 0-7502-0754-X

Typeset by DJS Fotoset Ltd, Brighton, Sussex
Printed and bound in Italy by L.E.G.O. S.p.A., Vicenza

Contents

Words that appear in **bold** in the text are explained in the glossary on page 32.

Colour everywhere

We live in a world full of colour.
How many colours can you see in this picture?

4

These poppies and fruits are very colourful.

The world would be a very dull place without any colour.

Colour in landscapes

During the day, the sky is usually blue. But in the evening, as the sun gets lower, the sky turns to yellow, orange and red. This is called a sunset.

These Cliffs in Utah (USA) have layers of different coloured rock.

Water has no colour, but when the sun shines, the water in some lakes looks bright blue, like this Canadian lake in the Rocky Mountains.

The **climate** can change the colour of the **landscape.** In cold parts of the world, snow and ice cover the land in a white blanket.

In hot, wet places there are lots and lots of plants, so the landscape is very green. This is the rainforest in Indonesia.

Deserts are found in hot, dry areas. They are usually very colourless places. Only one or two plants grow here, and there are very few animals. Can you think why?

Colourful seasons

The colours of the landscape change with the seasons. In spring and summer, the time of growth, plants are very green. In autumn, the leaves of trees change from green to yellow, red and gold. In winter, the land is sometimes covered with white snow.

The fields are full of flowers in spring.
How many different colours can you see?

Colour in plants

Most leaves are green but some leaves have other colours as well. Leaves that have white or yellow patches are called **variegated** leaves.

Flowers are brightly coloured to attract insects. This bee-fly is feeding on the marigold's **nectar.**

The pink and yellow colours of this flower tell the butterfly that there is plenty of sugary nectar for it to eat.

Animals on show

Birds and other animals are often brightly coloured. Sometimes the colours are arranged in patterns.

Many animals use colour to help them attract a **mate**. Some male birds, like this peacock, have beautifully coloured feathers.

People often like to keep fish because of their pretty colours and patterns.

Hiding with colour

The golden fur of this lioness helps her to blend in with the background, so that she can creep up on her **prey** without being seen. This is called **camouflage.**

Other animals use camouflage to hide from their **predators.** This lizard is the same colour as the ground so it is difficult to see.

16

The ringed plover lays her eggs among the pebbles. There are three eggs in this picture. Can you spot them?

Colour in food

The bright colours of these vegetables and fruit make them look good to eat!

18

This plate of paella is full of colour!   It is a popular meal in Spain.

Sweets also come in many colours and shapes.

Colourful clothes

Members of a sport's team all wear the same colour. How does this help the team?

◀ These Japanese girls are wearing modern and **traditional** clothes. The **kimono** is more colourful than the skirt and top.

These colourful clothes are ▶ worn to celebrate a Hindu wedding in a Sri Lankan temple.

Colourful materials

Plastics come in all shapes, sizes and colours. We use plastic to make many different things. How many plastic things can you find in your home?

Balloons are made from rubber in all sorts of colours!

Colour in the streets

Streets are bright, busy places. These American cheerleaders are celebrating New Year's Day in London .

In New York all the taxis are painted bright yellow so that they are very easy to spot in the crowded streets.

In the evenings, some streets are lit up with cheerful coloured lights.

The colours we see often have special meanings. What do the red, amber and green lights of traffic signals tell us?

Colour in art

These crayons come in many colours. Can you name them?

Artists use many different coloured paints. They mix them up to make new colours, like these children are doing.

If you have red, blue and yellow paint you can make any other colour except white and black.

There are many sorts of crayons, paints and felt-tips. Which ones do you have?

Warning colours

Bright colours are easy to see. Sometimes they are used to warn of danger. The yellow and black stripes of the wasp are warning colours. They warn you that the wasp may sting.

These caterpillars use colours to tell predators that they are **poisonous** to eat.

A fire engine is painted red to warn of danger. How else does it warn you of danger?

Notes for parents and teachers

Science and Technology
- Children should explore and talk about coloured materials and their properties so as to appreciate the variety of living things and materials in the environment.
- Experiments with smarties is a fun approach. (Tell colour by taste, smarties in water, smarties on blotting paper.)
- Put a black felt pen spot on filter paper and drop water on to the spot to achieve effective results.
- What happens when red cabbage is mixed with different things?
- Dip samples of cloth into dyes from plants. Mount and label.
- Isaac Newton experimented to see what happened if colours were spun fast. Make your own colour wheels.

Maths
- Problem solving and investigations e.g. How many different ways can you colour the clown's three buttons using two or three colours?
- Colour and pattern. Stick a small pattern sample in the middle of a piece of paper and continue the pattern all over the paper.
- Design your own wallpaper or fabric design.
- Sorting and classifying according to colour.

Language
- Encourage descriptive language when describing results and interpreting observations of experiments.
- Story and poetry writing – colour and moods/feelings.
- Fiction stories with colour as their theme: – *Emily's paintbox* by Riana Duncan (Pub. Andre Deutsch), *A colour of his own* by Leo Lionni (Pub. Picture Lions), *The day it rained colours* by Roy Etherton (Pub. Lions), *Mr Rabbit and the lovely present* by C. Zolotow (Pub. Bodley Head), *Mr Rabbit helps a little girl find things of her mother's favourite colour.*

History and Geography
- Concept of change and new/old can be explored. Animals change colour as they grow, e.g. grey cygnets become white swans and green caterpillars become colourful butterflies.
- Colours and symbols used in road signs. Experiment with which colours show up best. Chart results.
- Make a fog box using a cardboard box and layers of tracing paper. How many layers of tracing paper need removing before you can see the object in the box?
- Look for rainbows on the edge of mirrors and in foam bubbles.

Art/Craft
Bring light and colour into the classroom by making stained glass tissue paper windows.
- Make a shade chart from light → dark. Mount together with paper/cloth samples which match the colours.

Personal and Social Education
- Favourite colours and colours in your home. Also discuss the issue of colour and sex stereotypes (blue for boys, pink for girls).
- Examine the skin closely – is white skin really white? Also discuss the harmful effects of over exposure to the sun.

Music/Dance/Drama
- Colours and moods can be reflected through music and movement.
- Learn songs and act scenes from the story of *Joseph and his Amazing Technicolour Dreamcoat.*

30

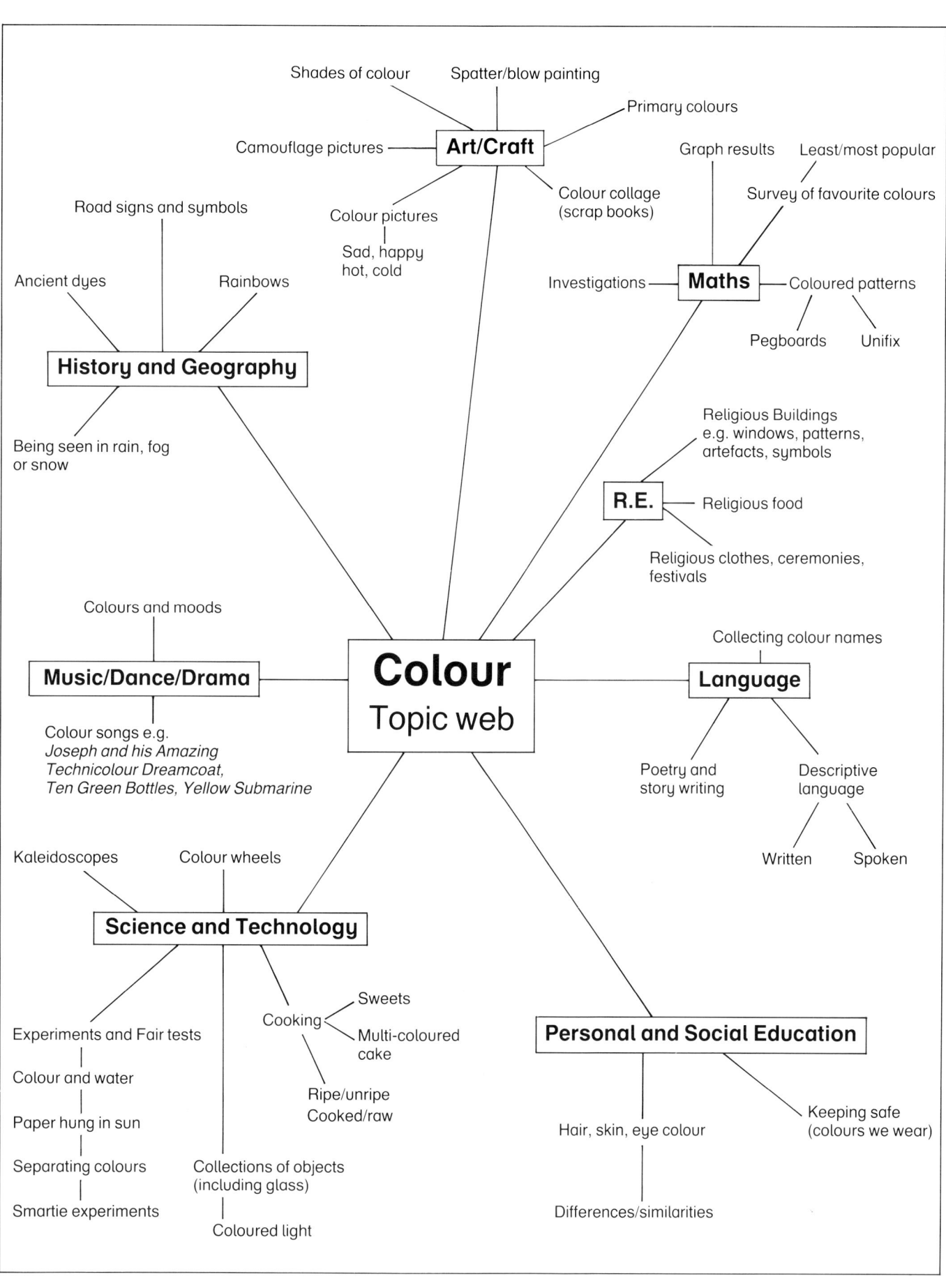

Glossary

Camouflage An animal's shape or colour that makes it difficult to see.

Climate The weather of a place or country.

Kimono Long, loose robe, worn in Japan.

Landscape The shape and features of the land.

Mate An animal's partner.

Nectar A sweet, sugary substance produced by flowers.

Poisonous Something that will make you sick.

Predators Animals that hunt and feed on other animals.

Prey An animal that is hunted and eaten by another animal.

Traditional Following customs from the past.

Variegated A leaf that is green and white.

Index